SCHOLASTIC
ENGLISH SKILLS

Handwriting
Workbook

Ages 4–7

SCHOLASTIC
ENGLISH SKILLS

Handwriting

Book End, Range Road, Witney, Oxfordshire, OX29 0YD
www.scholastic.co.uk

© 2015, Scholastic Ltd

3456789   8901234

British Library Cataloguing-in-Publication Data
A catalogue record for this book is available from the British Library.

ISBN 978-1407-14170-1
Printed by Ashford Colour Press

Due to the nature of the web we cannot guarantee the content or links of
any site mentioned. We strongly recommend that teachers check websites
before using them in the classroom.

Every effort has been made to trace copyright holders for the works
reproduced in this book, and the publishers apologise for any inadvertent
omissions.

Author
Amanda McLeod

Editorial
Rachel Morgan, Anna Hall, Vicky Butt, Jo Kemp

Cover and Series Design
Nicolle Thomas and Neil Salt

Series consultant
Amanda McLeod

Design
Anna Oliwa

Illustration
Cathy Hughes

Cover Illustration
Eddie Rego

Lenny illustration
Paul Hutchinson

Contents

How to use this book

● *Scholastic English Skills Workbooks* help your child to practise and improve their skills in English.

● The content is divided into topics. Find out what your child is doing in school, and dip into the practice activities as required.

● Keep the working time short, and come back to an activity if your child finds it too difficult. Ask your child to note any areas of difficulty. Don't worry if your child does not 'get' a concept first time, as children learn at different rates and content is likely to be covered at different times throughout the school year.

● Find out more information about handwriting and check your child's answers at www.scholastic.co.uk/ses/handwriting.

● Give lots of encouragement, complete the 'How did you do' for each activity and the progress chart as your child finishes each chapter.

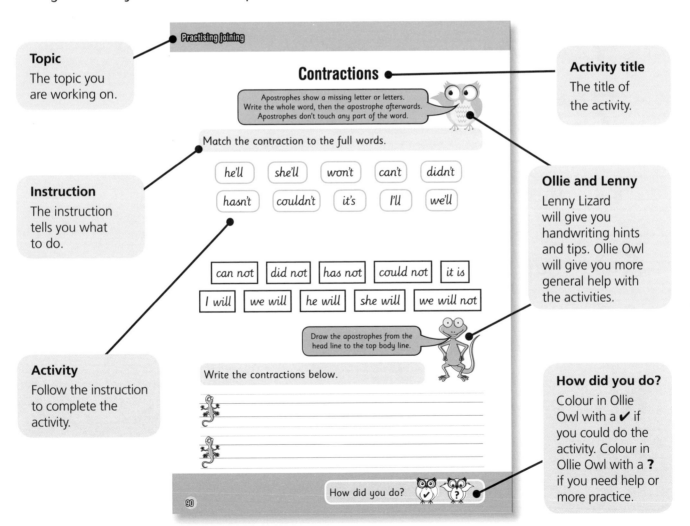

Topic
The topic you are working on.

Instruction
The instruction tells you what to do.

Activity
Follow the instruction to complete the activity.

Activity title
The title of the activity.

Ollie and Lenny
Lenny Lizard will give you handwriting hints and tips. Ollie Owl will give you more general help with the activities.

How did you do?
Colour in Ollie Owl with a ✔ if you could do the activity. Colour in Ollie Owl with a ? if you need help or more practice.

Practising joining

Contractions

Apostrophes show a missing letter or letters. Write the whole word, then the apostrophe afterwards. Apostrophes don't touch any part of the word.

Match the contraction to the full words.

| he'll | she'll | won't | can't | didn't |
| hasn't | couldn't | it's | I'll | we'll |

| can not | did not | has not | could not | it is |
| I will | we will | he will | she will | we will not |

Draw the apostrophes from the head line to the top body line.

Write the contractions below.

How did you do?

90

If you need help, ask an adult!

Size

Lenny Lizard appears on tramlines to support letter formation. His 'head', 'body' and 'tail' act as reminders for letter size.

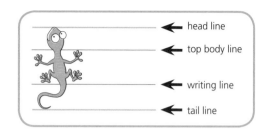

head line
top body line
writing line
tail line

Shape names

Letters are grouped into different shapes, as described below.

- Straight down letters (i, j, l, t, u, y) – start with a 'straight down' stroke.

- Down, up and over letters (b, h, k, m, n, p, r) – start with drawing down, back-up along the same line and then arching over to the right.

- Up, backwards and around letters (a, c, d, e, f, g, o, q, s) – start at 1 o'clock and go up, backwards and around.

- Zooming letters (v, w, x, z) – start with straight zig-zagged lines.

End positions

Letters can end in two positions.

- End-low letters (a, b, c, d, e, f, g, h, i, j, k, l, m, n, p, q, s, t, u, x, y, z) – end on or below the writing line.

- End-high letters (o, r, v, w) – end on the top body line.

Joins

Joining is taking your pen from the end of one letter to the start of the next. There are three different main types of join:

- Diagonal joins – from the end of a letter, diagonally up to the next letter. Formed with end-low or end-high letters.

- Drop-on joins – from the end of a letter, dropping onto an up, backwards and around shape (take your pen over to one o'clock). Formed with end-low or end-high letters.

- Horizontal joins (o, r, v, w) – from the end of a letter, straight across to the next letter. Formed with end-high letters.

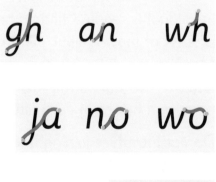

Handedness

This series supports right-handed and left-handed children. We suggest that left-handers adopt a slightly italic style of script so that it is more comfortable when writing down, up and over letters, and up, backwards and around letters. Teaching left-handers how to sit, position the paper and form letters correctly, should negate any problems.

Sit left-handers to the left of right-handers, or next to another left-hander. This will ensure their elbows don't bump together.

For more information about this series and exercises you can do to support your child's writing development, please see the website www.scholastic.co.uk/ses/handwriting.

● Right-handed alphabet   ● Left-handed alphabet

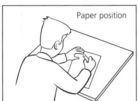

● Right-handed pen grip and paper position   ● Left-handed pen grip and paper position

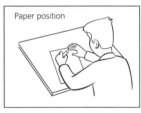

Joining

This series encourages children to begin joining from Reception, but only when each individual is ready. Children believe joining is difficult; it is not. Joining is the simple process of moving your pen from where one letter ends to where the next one starts. Most joining difficulties are removed if children are told to 'move from the end of that letter to the start of the next'. Using the terminology above helps to identify the start point and height of each letter (Lenny's body, shape names, ending positions and joins).

Do not introduce joining until letter formation is secure; incorrect formation hinders the acquisition of legibility, especially at speed. To judge this, it is important to see a child actually writing, as, once written, it is hard to ascertain how a letter was formed. Some children with weaker visual perception and motor skills may not be able to join, but all effort should be given towards building up this perceptual and motor strength first, before taking that decision (refer to the website for exercises).

Straight down shapes

Keep your lines straight and parallel.
Make your exits smooth, not sharp.

Trace over the patterns.

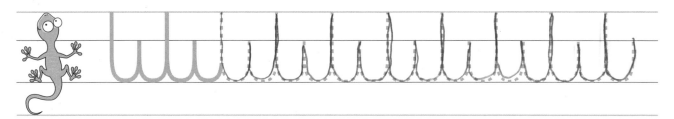

Write the straight down patterns. Join the dots.

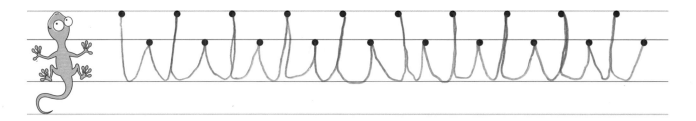

Write your own straight down patterns.

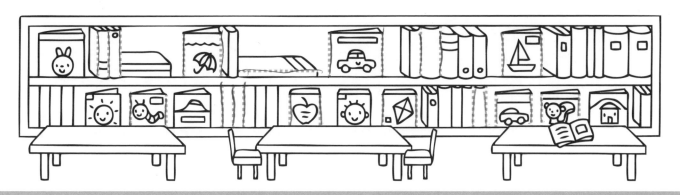

How did you do?

Down, up and over shapes

Make your curves round. Keep your lines straight and parallel. Go from the top body line to the writing line.

Trace over the patterns and then practise writing your own.

Trace over the curves to complete Lenny's vegetable patch.

How did you do?

Up, backwards and around shapes

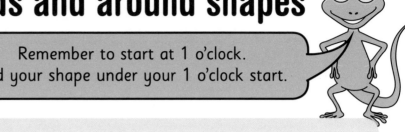

Remember to start at 1 o'clock.
End your shape under your 1 o'clock start.

Trace over the curves and then write your own curves.

Trace over the curves to complete the Viking ship picture.

How did you do?

Zooming shapes

Make each zigzag straight and the same width apart. No line should be straight up or straight down (vertical).

Trace over the zooming shapes from the top body line to the writing line.

Join the dots and then write your own zooming shapes.

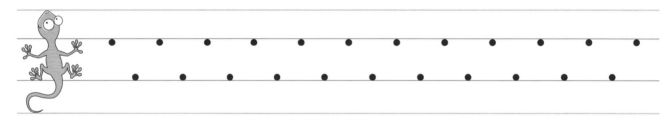

How did you do?

Letters s, a, t, p

Trace over the letters and then write some of your own.

a ·   s ·

t ·   p ·

Trace over the word and match it to the picture.

pasta

tap

past

Letters s, a, t, p

Keep your line straight for down, up and over **p**.
Cross your **t** at the top body line.

Write **s**, **a**, **t** and **p** on the line below.

Trace over the **s**, **a**, **t** and **p** in the words below.

are

truck

sun

pin

tin

pen

roar

pest

How did you do?

Letters i, n, m, d

Start at 1 o'clock for up, backwards and around **d**.
Make sure you dot your **i** above the top body line.

Trace over the letters and then write some of your own.

i ·   n ·

m ·   d ·

Trace over the word and match it to the picture.

mind

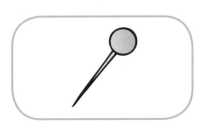

pin

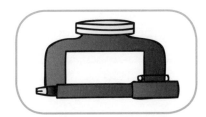

ink

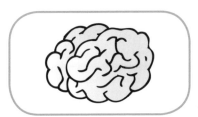

Letters i, n, m, d

Make sure both arches of your **m** are the same height.
Draw parallel straight lines for down, up and over **n** and **m**.

Write **i**, **n**, **m** and **d** on the line below.

Look at the pictures. Do the words start with **m**, **i**, **n** or **d**?
Write the letter.

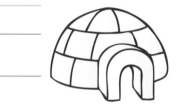

Trace this word. Then copy it.

digger

How did you do?

Letters g, o, c, k

Keep the circle of your **k** under the top body line.
Say "I want to be a **b**. Oh bother, I've become a **k**!"

Trace over the letters and then write some of your own.

 g · o ·

 c · k ·

Trace over the word and match it to the picture.

 king

goat

ogre

Letters g, o, c, k

Start at 1 o'clock for up, backwards and around **c**, **g** and **o**.
Keep your **o** round and finish at 1 o'clock.

Write **g**, **o**, **c** and **k** on the line below.

_____

Find and trace the **g**, **o**, **c** and **k** letters in the fruit picture.

grapes   oranges

kiwis   cherries

Trace this word. Then copy it.

knock

How did you do?

Letters e, u, r, h

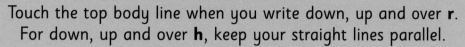
Touch the top body line when you write down, up and over **r**.
For down, up and over **h**, keep your straight lines parallel.

Trace over the letters and then write some of your own.

 e.   u

 r.   h

Trace over the word and match it to the picture.

thunder

earth

herd

How did you do?

Letters e, u, r, h

Keep your straight lines parallel for straight down **u**.
Finish **e** just above the writing line, under 1 o'clock.

Write **e**, **u**, **r** and **h** on the line below.

Look at the pictures. Do the words start with **e**, **u**, **r** or **h**?
Write the letter.

Trace this word. Then copy it.

under

How did you do?

Letters b, f, l, j, q

b and **l** start at the top on the head line.
f, **j** and **q** all go down to the tail line.
Make sure you dot your **j** above the top body line.

Trace over the letters and then write some of your own.

b   f

l   j   q

Trace over the word and match it to the picture.

flea

jumble

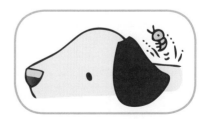

quilt

How did you do?

Letters b, f, l, j, q

Up, backwards and around **f** starts at 1 o'clock.
f is a straight letter. It only curves at the very top and very bottom.

Write **b**, **f**, **l**, **j** and **q** on the line below.

_____

Write the answers across to complete the puzzle.

1.

2.

3.

4.

5.

1. b
2. l
3. a
4. c
5. k

How did you do?

Letters v, w, x, y, z

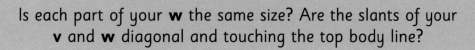

Is each part of your **w** the same size? Are the slants of your **v** and **w** diagonal and touching the top body line?

Trace over the letters and then write some of your own.

v ·   w ·

x ·   y ·   z ·

Trace over the word and match it to the picture.

vest

yell

well

zoom

fox

Letters v, w, x, y, z

Sit the body part of the **y** on the writing line.
Draw a rectangle around **x** and **z**. Do the letters touch each corner?

Write **v**, **w**, **x**, **y** and **z** on the line below.

_____

Look at the pictures. Do the words have a **v**, **w**, **x**, **y** or **z** in them? Write the letter.

  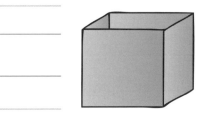

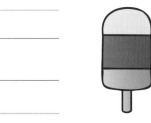 

Trace this word. Then copy it.

 *wavy*

How did you do?

Capital A and B

Are your **A** diagonals slanting?
Are the two circles of your **B** the same size?

Trace over the lower-case **a** and **b** and the capital **A** and **B**. Then write some of your own.

 a ● A ●

 b ● B ●

Write **A** and **B** on the line below.

Complete the sentences by adding the capital letter.

___pril comes after March.

___pril comes before May.

___ring the stuff here!

___ye bye Bob!

How did you do?

Capital C and D

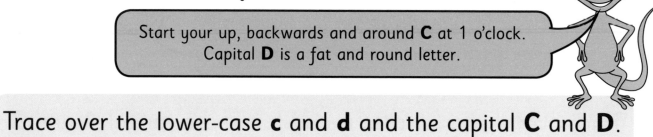

Start your up, backwards and around **C** at 1 o'clock.
Capital **D** is a fat and round letter.

Trace over the lower-case **c** and **d** and the capital **C** and **D**.
Then write some of your own.

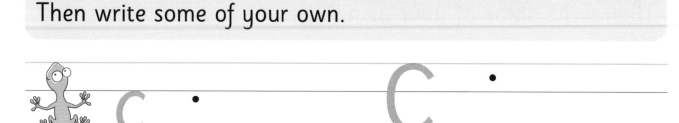

c · C ·

d · D ·

Write **C** and **D** on the line below.

_____

Complete the names below.

| ___hris | ___erek |

| ___arol | ___onna |

How did you do?

Capital E and F

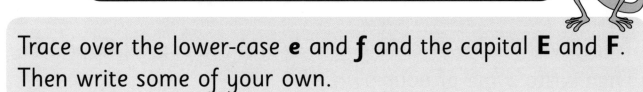

Are your **E** horizontals straight?
Are your **F** horizontals on the head line and top body line?

Trace over the lower-case **e** and **f** and the capital **E** and **F**. Then write some of your own.

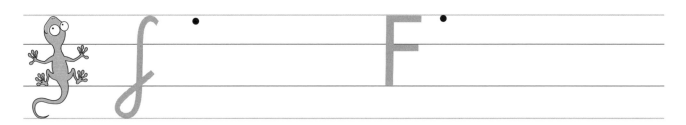

Write **E** and **F** on the line below.

Trace over the letters to complete the library scene.

Capital G and H

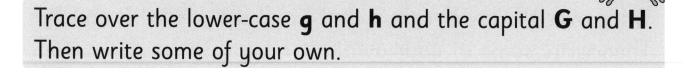

Start your **G** at 1 o'clock. Are the straight lines of your **H** vertical, and is the horizontal on the top body line?

Trace over the lower-case **g** and **h** and the capital **G** and **H**. Then write some of your own.

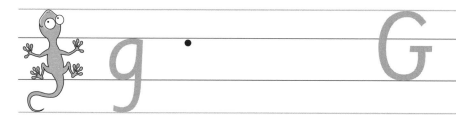

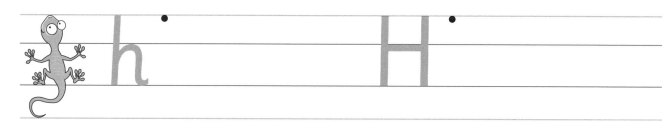

Write **G** and **H** on the line below.

_____

Complete the words to find out which countries these are.

___ermany

___reece

___olland

___ungary

How did you do?

26

Capital I and J

Capital **I** and **J** do not have a dot.
Capital **J** sits on the writing line.

Trace over the lower-case **i** and **j** and the capital **I** and **J**.
Then write some of your own.

Write **I** and **J** on the line below.

_____

Complete the sentences by adding the capital letter.

___ went to ___ndia.

___ saw volcanoes in ___celand.

___ack and ___ill went up the hill.

___anuary, ___une and ___uly begin with a capital J.

How did you do?

Capital K and L

Do your **K** diagonals meet at the top body line?
Is the horizontal line of your **L** straight and on the writing line?

Trace over the lower-case **k** and **l** and the capital **K** and **L**.
Then write some of your own.

Write **K** and **L** on the line below.

Trace over the letters to complete the ducks.

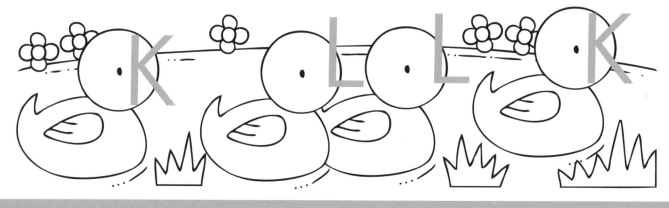

How did you do?

Capital M and N

M has two parallel straight lines and a small middle **v**.
The diagonal of your **N** goes from the top left to bottom right.

Trace over the lower-case **m** and **n** and the capital **M** and **N**.
Then write some of your own.

 m  M

 n N

Write **M** and **N** on the line below.

_____

Complete the sentences by adding the capital letter.

___ay is the month between April and June.

___ount Everest is the highest in the world.

___ovember is the beginning of winter.

___ovember is the month between October and December.

How did you do?

Capital O and P

Does your up, backwards and around **O** start at 1 o'clock?
Start the **P** circle at the head line and end just below the top body line.

Trace over the lower-case **o** and **p** and the capital **O** and **P**.
Then write some of your own.

Write **O** and **P** on the line below.

_____

Complete the sentences by adding the capital letter.

___ctober is the month after September

___ctober is the month before November.

___liver, shall we go to Portugal or Peru?

___lease may we go to Paris next holiday?

How did you do?

Capital Q and R

Start your up, backwards and around **Q** at 1 o'clock.
Start the **R** circle at the head line and end just below the top body line.

Trace over the lower-case **q** and **r** and the capital **Q** and **R**. Then write some of your own.

Write **Q** and **R** on the line below.

Trace over the letters to complete the bicycle race.

Capital S and T

Write **S** with equal-sized circles and start at 1 o'clock.
Is the horizontal line of your **T** straight and on the head line?

Trace over the lower-case **s** and **t** and the capital **S** and **T**.
Then write some of your own.

Write **S** and **T** on the line below.

_____

Complete the words to find out which countries these are.

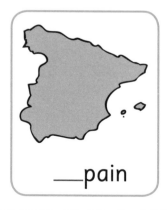

| ___pain | ___witzerland | ___urkey | ___hailand |

How did you do?

Capital U and V

Capital **U** does not have an exit stroke and the verticals are straight. Are the slants of your capital **V** diagonal?

Trace over the lower-case **u** and **v** and the capital **U** and **V**. Then write some of your own.

Write **U** and **V** on the line below.

Complete the sentences by adding the capital letter.

____niforms are often worn at school.

____iolet plays the violin very well.

"____ictory is ours!" said the school team.

____nless Ursula is good she will be sent to bed.

How did you do?

Capital W and X

Draw a rectangle around **X**. Do you touch each corner?
Are the slants of your **W** diagonal? Is each part the same size?

Trace over the lower-case **w** and **x** and the capital **W** and **X**.
Then write some of your own.

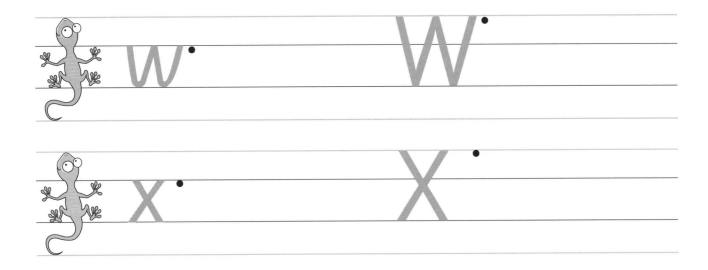

Write **W** and **X** on the line below.

_____

Trace the letters to complete the oxen and water troughs.

How did you do?

Capital Y and Z

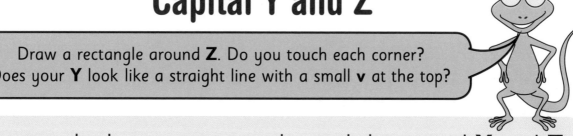

Draw a rectangle around **Z**. Do you touch each corner?
Does your **Y** look like a straight line with a small **v** at the top?

Trace over the lower-case **y** and **z** and the capital **Y** and **Z**.
Then write some of your own.

y ·   Y ·

z ·   Z ·

Write **Y** and **Z** on the line below.

_____

Complete the sentences by adding the capital letter.

___esterday, Younes yelped.

"___ou must tell the truth!" said my teacher.

"___ap!" went the laser gun in the cartoon.

"___zz," snoozed the sleepy zebra in the zoo.

How did you do?

Number 1

Trace over the big number, dot and word.
Then complete the lines.

one

Count the number of oranges and write the number on the lines.

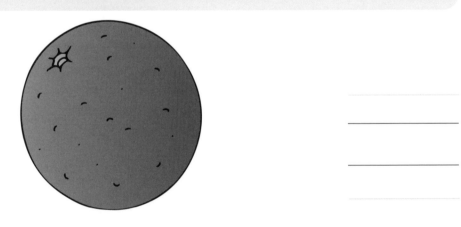

Write your own number 1 on the line.

How did you do?

Number 2

Trace over the big number, dots and word.
Then complete the lines.

2

two

Count the number of turtles and write the number on the lines.

Write your own number 2 on the line.

How did you do?

Number 3

Trace over the big number, dots and word.
Then complete the lines.

3

three

Count the number of trees and write the number on the lines.

Write your own number 3 on the line.

How did you do?

Number 4

Trace over the big number, dots and word.
Then complete the lines.

Count the number of feathers and write the number on the lines.

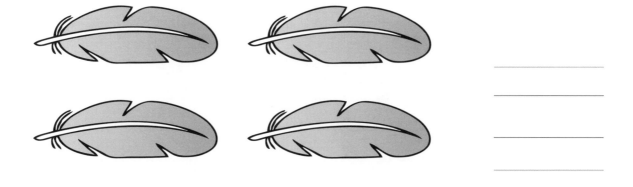

Write your own number 4 on the line.

How did you do?

Number 5

Trace over the big number, dots and word.
Then complete the lines.

five

Count the number of fires and write the number on the lines.

Write your own number 5 on the line.

How did you do?

Number 6

Trace over the big number, dots and word.
Then complete the lines.

six

Count the number of choirboys and write the number on the lines.

Write your own number 6 on the line.

How did you do?

Number 7

Trace over the big number, dots and word.
Then complete the lines.

seven

Count the number of sea horses and write the number on the lines.

Write your own number 7 on the line.

How did you do?

Number 8

Trace over the big number, dots and word.
Then complete the lines.

eight

Count the number of elephants and write the number on the lines.

Write your own number 8 on the line.

How did you do?

Number 9

Trace over the big number, dots and word.
Then complete the lines.

9

nine

Count the number of Lenny Lizards and write the number on the lines.

Write your own number 9 on the line.

How did you do?

Number 10

Trace over the big number, dots and word.
Then complete the lines.

Count the number of tigers and write the number on the lines.

Write your own number 10 on the line.

How did you do?

Alternative forms: new e

Start from your join for the new form of **e**.
Use the new **e** in the middle of words.

Trace over the different forms of **e** and then write some of your own.

Trace over the word and match it to the picture.

engine

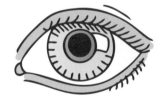

eye

eel

How did you do?

Alternative forms: new e

Make both your new and old **e** round.

Write your old and new **e** on the lines below.

_____

_____

Read the sentences below and trace over the old and new **e** words. Match the sentence to the picture.

I see the elephant.

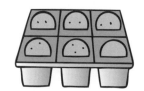

I like eggs for tea.

My brother is eight.

How did you do?

Alternative forms: new s

New **s**: From 12 o'clock (not 1) go back down a tiny bit and do a BIG circle.

Trace the different forms of **s**. Then write some of your own.

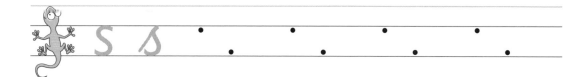

Trace over the new and old **s** in the words below.

seals

sweets

glasses

shells

circles

balls

sisters

scissors

soldiers

How did you do?

Alternative forms: new s

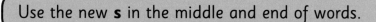

Use the new **s** in the middle and end of words.

Write your old and new **s** on the lines below.

_____

_____

Read the sentences below and trace over the new and old **s**.
Match the sentence to the picture.

Ben has an easel
to paint.

Wash your sticky
fingers!

Sharks swim in
seas.

How did you do?

End-low diagonal joins: ur

> Make your exit stroke smooth.
> Go from the end of a letter to the start of the next.

Trace over the **ur** and then write some of your own.

ur

Read the words. Trace over the **ur** join and match it to the picture.

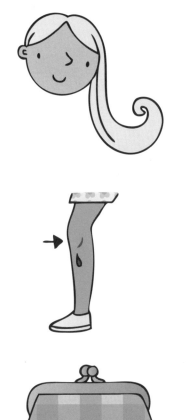

hurt

burst

curl

nurse

church

purse

How did you do?

End-low diagonal joins: ll

Make your exit stroke smooth.
Don't write the next letter on top of the first.

Trace over the **ll** and then write some of your own.

ll

Read the word and trace **ll**. Draw pictures of the words and draw lines to match those that rhyme.

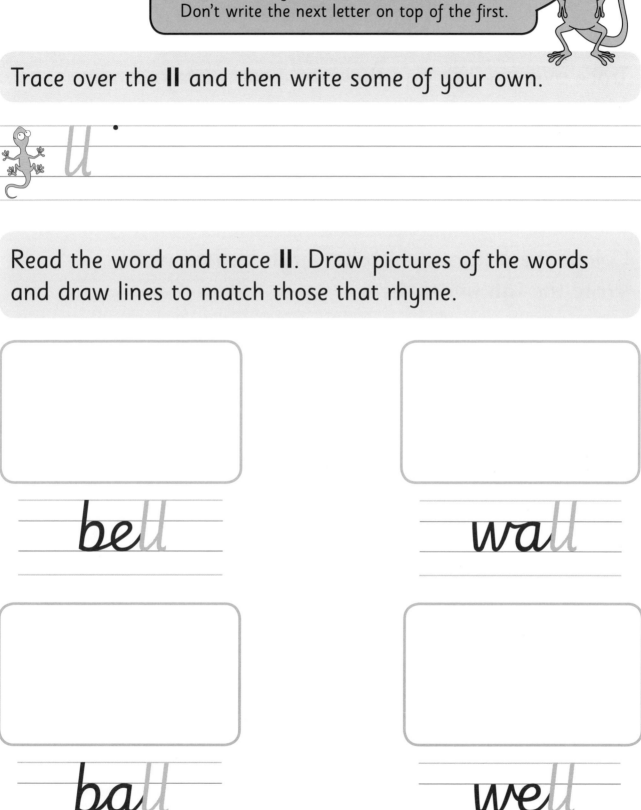

bell

wall

ball

well

How did you do?

End-low drop-on joins: igh

> Dot your **i** at the end. Exit your **g** on the writing line. Then go to the start of the **h**.

Trace over the **igh** and then write some of your own.

 *igh*

Colour the pictures which have **igh** in their word.
Write the **igh** under them.

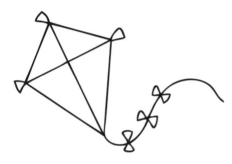

How did you do?

End-low drop-on joins: ng

Go from the end of **n** and drop onto the 1 o'clock **g**.
Make your exit stroke smooth.

Trace over the **ng** and then write some of your own.

ng

Find the picture that ends with **ng**. Trace over the **ng** joins and then colour in the **ng** shapes.

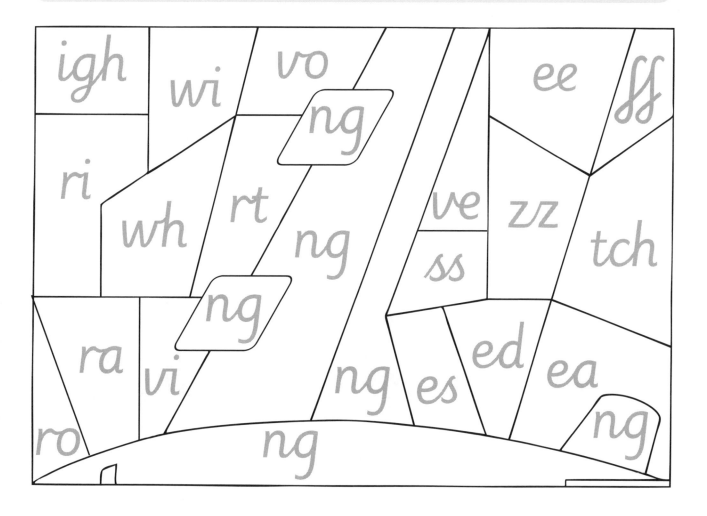

How did you do?

End-high horizontal joins: wi

End your **w** on the top body line.
Keep your **w** exit a straight line.

Trace over the joined **wi** and then write some of your own.

 *wi*

Write the word under the correct picture.

| wing | win | swim | swing | witch | wind |

How did you do?

54

End-high horizontal joins: vi and ri

v and **r** are end-high letters. Keep your **v** exit a horizontal line and curl your **r** exit up to the top body line.

Trace over the joined **vi** and **ri**.
Then write some of your own.

vi ·   *ri* ·

Trace the border with **vi** and **ri**.
Read the words. Copy them below.

rise view ripe vile

End-high diagonal joins: wh

Finish your letter first before drawing the join. End your **w** on the top body line. Don't write the next letter on top of the first.

Trace over the joined **wh** and then write some of your own.

wh

Write the words to complete the sentences. Then draw a line to the correct picture.

who   *what*   *when*   *which*

I said _____ you were.

I asked _____ you were reading.

I asked _____ we should go.

I asked _____ jumper to wear.

How did you do?

End-high diagonal joins: rt

Don't write the next letter on top of the first. Don't dip your **r** and make an **n**. Cross your **t** at the end.

Trace over the joined **rt** and then write some of your own.

 *rt .*

Trace over the **rt** joins. Draw lines to match the words that rhyme.

art

fort

dirt

alert

hurt

yoghurt

advert

skirt

sort

cart

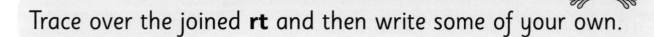

How did you do?

End-high drop-on joins: ra and ro

Don't dip your **r** and make **n**. **r** ends high and drops onto **a** and **o** to start at 1 o'clock.

Trace over the joined **ra** and **ro**.
Then write some of your own.

ra

ro

Read this sentence. Underline the **ra** and **ro** words and rewrite the sentence below.

Around and round the ragged rock the ragged rascal ran.

Try saying the sentence really quickly.

How did you do?

End-high drop-on joins: vo

End your **v** at the top body line. Keep your exit horizontal and drop onto **o** at 1 o'clock.

Trace over the joined **vo** and then write some of your own.

vo

Write these **vo** words around the volcano.

vole   convoy   voice   vote   ivory   flavour

How did you do?

End-high to e: ve

Drop from the exit of the **v** to the start of the **e**. Don't go too low.

Trace over the joined **ve** and then write some of your own.

ve

Read these **ve** words. Write seven of them in the hive.

vet	five	dive	hive	live
strive	arrive	avenue	eve	

How did you do?

End-high to e: we

Draw the **w** exit to the start of the **e**. Don't go too low.

Trace over the joined **we** and then write some of your own.

we

Read the sentences below. Underline the **we** words.
Write them below.

1. We went by boat past the seaweed.

2. A weatherman wears wellington boots when it rains for a whole week.

3. The spider wept when its web was washed away.

How did you do?

Tricky joins: ee

Finish your first **e** on the writing line, directly under 1 o'clock.
Don't sit your second **e** on top of the first. Give yourself more space.

Trace over the joined **ee** and then write some of your own.

ee .

Find the words with **ee** in the picture. Colour them in and then write them on the lines.

sheep   weeds   queen   jeep   bee   feet

How did you do?

Tricky joins: ff

Remember to start at 1 o'clock. Keep your **f** verticals straight. Don't add an extra crossbar for **f**. The join takes its place.

Trace over the joined **ff** and then write some of your own.

ff

Sort the Big Bad Wolf's words. Write them below.

| staff | cliff | toff | cuff | chaff | sniff |
| whiff | off | tiff | stuff | puff | scoff |

aff

iff

off

uff

How did you do?

Tricky joins: ss

Finish **s** under its joining stroke, not under the 12 o'clock mark.
Exit your first **s** along the line you have just drawn.

Trace over the joined **ss** and then write some of your own.

Read the sentence. Underline the **ss** words and rewrite them below.

The boss played chess with me but made a fuss and missed a go. "That was my loss," he cried.

How did you do?

Tricky joins: zz

Make sure your **z** horizontal lines are straight. Draw a square around each **z** to check it's right. **zz** has a diagonal join.

Trace over the joined **zz** and then write some of your own.

 zz

Write the word under the correct picture.

 jazz   fizz   frizz   whizz   buzz   pizza

How did you do?

tch

Feel the difference in **tch** and **ch** when you say them. Keep your **h** verticals parallel. Cross your **t** at the end.

Trace over the **tch** and then write a line of your own.

 *tch*

Write these words into the correct column.

| witch | beach | hutch | coach | watch |
| ostrich | peach | sandwich | switch | thatch |

ch	tch
1. _____	1. _____
2. _____	2. _____
3. _____	3. _____
4. _____	4. _____
5. _____	5. _____

How did you do?

s or es?

Use **es** if there are two beats in the word. Write **s** if the **s** sounds like **z**. Use the new styles of **e** and **s**.

Trace over the **es** and then write some of your own.

 es

Write these words into the correct column.

| cats | fans | misses | classes | rocks |
| nests | matches | dogs | roses | boxes |

s	es
1. _____	1. _____
2. _____	2. _____
3. _____	3. _____
4. _____	4. _____
5. _____	5. _____

How did you do?

ed

Trace over the **ed** and then write some of your own.

 *ed*

Say the present tense of these words to your teacher.
Does the spelling of these root words change?

These **ed** words have different sounds.
Write them into the correct column.

blinked   walked   hunted   fizzed   played
enjoyed   printed   painted   jumped

t	d	
1. _____	1. _____	4. _____
2. _____	2. _____	5. _____
3. _____	3. _____	6. _____

How did you do?

Magic vowels

Magic vowels send their magic over the consonant, hit the vowel on the head and make it shout out its alphabet name.

Read these words and write them into the correct column. The first two have been done for you.

rid   ride   cube   time   plan   hop
tube   cub   kit   Tim   kite   plane
cute   slid   hope   slide   cut   tub

no magic vowel	with magic vowel
slid	slide
rid	ride

How did you do?

ea

What two sounds do these **ea** letters make?
Use the new style of **e** and drop onto 1 o'clock for **a**.

Trace over the **ea** and then write some of your own.

ea

Find these **ea** words in the picture. Colour the **ea** pictures and write the words as labels.

read	treasure	dream	tea
beach	sea	feather	bread

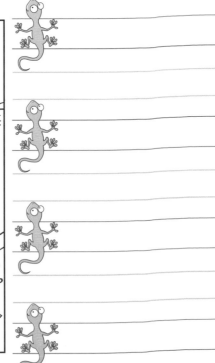

How did you do?

ir and ur

> **ur** and **ir** have the same sound. If in doubt, use **ur** for days and in the middle. Use **ir** for girls, numbers and circles.

Underline the **ur** and **ir** words. Write them below.

1. At Sports Day on Thursday, I came first and third.

2. The bird hurt its wing.

3. Each button burst when I was at the circus.

4. The nurse bandaged the burn on my arm.

5. At our school girls wear skirts and shirts.

How did you do?

ue and ew

ue and ew are more common than oo.
Exit your zooming w high and use the new style of e.

Read these words and complete the sentences.

| grew | blue | clue | flew | Tuesday |

1. Solve the _____.

2. The sea is _____.

3. After Monday is _____.

4. The bird _____ away.

5. The plant _____ up the wall.

What is the common sound? What two ways can you write it here?

_____ + _____ = _____

How did you do?

aw and au

Make sure your **u** verticals are parallel.
Drop onto 1 o'clock for your up, backwards and around **a**.

Read these words and write them under the correct picture.

paw   gnaw   draw   yawn   crawl
dinosaur   astronaut   sauce   autumn

How did you do? ✔ ?

y

No English word ends in the sound **i** (igloo) or **ee** (eek) when you can hear it. Use **y** instead, but do not exit the **y** with a loop. Make your **y** verticals parallel.

Read the sentences. Underline the **y** words and copy them.

1. The funny clown made me very happy at the family party.

2. I ate raspberry ice cream and drank frothy strawberry milkshake very quickly.

Can you think of two more **y** words like these?
Write the words and draw a picture of each.

How did you do?

ph

The **f** sound is not usually spelled as **ph** in short everyday words.
How many syllables does each **ph** and **f** word have?

Match these words to their picture and copy them out.

F

fat   filled   frog   foot   off

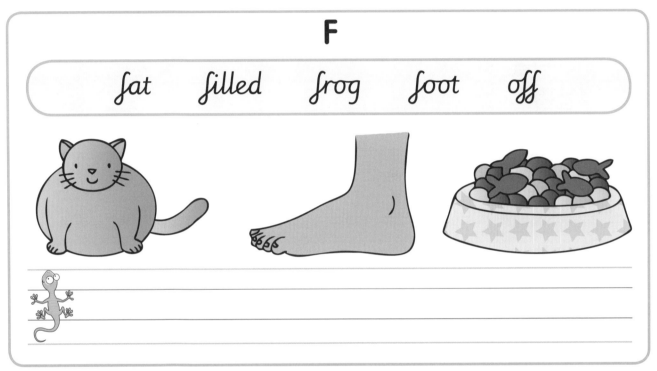

PH

alphabet   dolphin   elephant   phantom   trophy

How did you do?

k

We write **k** for the **k** sound when it is followed by **e**, **i** or **y**.
Keep the circle of your **k** under the top body line.

Are they **k** or **c** words? Write the correct word for each picture. Then circle **k** or **c**.

k / c

k / c

k / c

k / c

k / c

k / c

k / c

How did you do?

un

Make sure the verticals of your **u** and **n** are parallel.
The prefix **un** means 'not'.

Write **un** on the lines to complete the key.

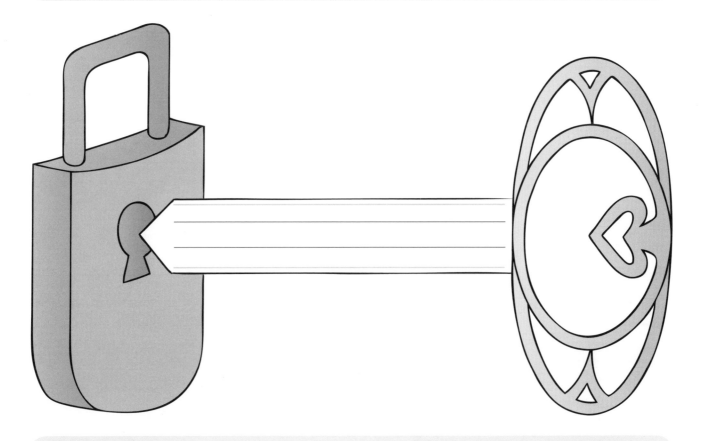

Write these words below.

| unhappy | undo | unload | unlock |

How did you do?

ear and are

What sounds do these words make?
we and **re** are tricky joins. Use the old style of **e**.

Write these words and draw a line to the picture.

tear bear pear wear bare dare share scared

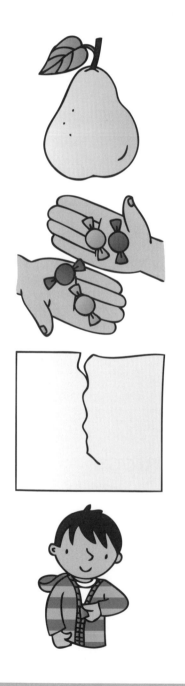

Compound words and syllable division

Compound words are joined words that would make sense on their own. A syllable is a breath, or a beat, in a word. Clap out syllables to count them.

Match these words to make new words and copy them out.

sun	room
bed	set
foot	berry
black	ball

How many syllables are in these words? Write the numbers.

picnic ☐   carrot ☐

pocket ☐   thunder ☐

rabbits ☐   ketchup ☐

How did you do?

ce, ci and cy

c followed by **e**, **i** or **y** makes a **sss** sound.
c has fallen in love with **e**, **i** and **y** and is a real softy.

Read these words and write them in the correct column.

| race | collar | cone | cut | city | circus |
| pencil | cup | cyclone | cap | cot | fancy |

Hard c	Soft c (sss sound)
1. _____	1. _____
2. _____	2. _____
3. _____	3. _____
4. _____	4. _____
5. _____	5. _____
6. _____	6. _____

How did you do?

kn, gn and wr

Can you hear the **k** in **kn**, the **w** in **wr** and the **g** in **gn**?
These words come from old English.

Read these words and find two of them in each picture.
Copy the words out next to the correct picture.

knocking   gnat   knee   writing   gnawing   wrong

How did you do?

el and le

Every syllable needs a vowel, even if you can't hear it. **el** words and **le** words are said differently. Can you hear them?

Draw a line from the syllables in the first column to the syllables in the second column to make a real word.
Then copy out the words in joined writing.

cam	ble	
ta	el	
ap	ple	
trav	nel	
bot	dle	
tun	el	
mid	tle	

es

Change **y** to **i** before adding **es** because **y** in the middle makes a **yu** sound, not **i**. Use the new style of **e** and **s**.

Match the singular word to its plural.

| fly | try | reply | copy | baby | carry |

| replies | carries | flies | babies | tries | copies |

Copy the word pairs.

The drop e rule

A suffix is a letter or letters added onto the end of a root word. Drop the end **e** from a root word when you add a vowel suffix.

Read these root words. Add the suffix. Then write the correct whole word in the column.

Root word	Suffix: ed, ing, er, est, y	Whole word
nice	est	_____
bike	er	_____
hope	ed	_____
drive	ing	_____
shine	y	_____
whine	y	_____
smile	ed	_____
dine	ing	_____
bake	er	_____
wise	est	_____

How did you do?

ta p ped

The doubling rule

Magic vowels can only jump over one consonant at a time. So, if you do not want the vowel to be changed, double the consonant after the vowel. The letter **k** is never doubled, use **ck** instead. The letter **x** is also never doubled.

Add suffixes to these root words. Use the new words to complete the sentences.

| tap | drop | run | fat | skip |

1. I _____ the nail into the wall.

2. I _____ the keys.

3. That _____ is fast.

4. The brown dog is the _____.

5. I like _____.

How did you do?

o

What two sounds does the letter **o** make here?
o has an end-high join.

Read the words and write them in the boxes below.

other   mother   operation   bottle   nothing
Monday   hospital   cotton   brother

o as in 'glove'

_____

_____

_____

_____

o as in 'cot'

_____

_____

_____

_____

How did you do?

qua and squa

What vowel sound do you hear after **qu** and **squa**?
Exit your **q** at the tail line.

Copy these words below the correct picture.

> quantity squat squabble quarry quarantine
> squad quality squash squalor

   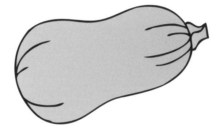 

1. _____   2. _____   3. _____

4. _____   5. _____   6. _____

7. _____   8. _____   9. _____

How did you do? ✔ ?

wa, war and wor

What vowel sound do you hear in **wa**? What vowel sounds do you hear after **w** in **war** and **w** in **wor**? End high after **w** and drop onto the **a** or **o**.

Read the sentences. Underline the **w** words and copy them. Then draw a picture.

1. Wanda the Wicked Witch wanted to watch the swan in the water.

2. The swarm of wasps wandered towards the warm fire.

3. The bookworm worked hard at reading the word world.

How did you do?

ment, less, ful, ness, ly

If a suffix starts with a consonant, add it straight onto the root word without changing the last letter. Change **y** to **i** in 2-syllable root words ending in consonant+**y**.

Split the root word from the suffix. The first two are done for you as an example.

enjoyment (sadness) careful playful hopeless plainness badly (merriment) happiness plentiful

root word	+	suffix
1. sad	+	ness
2. merry	+	ment
3.		
4.		
5.		
6.		
7.		
8.		
9.		
10.		

How did you do?

Contractions

Apostrophes show a missing letter or letters.
Write the whole word, then the apostrophe afterwards.
Apostrophes don't touch any part of the word.

Match the contraction to the full words.

| he'll | she'll | won't | can't | didn't |

| hasn't | couldn't | it's | I'll | we'll |

| can not | did not | has not | could not | it is |

| I will | we will | he will | she will | we will not |

Draw the apostrophes from the head line to the top body line.

Write the contractions below.

How did you do?

Possessive apostrophe

A possessive apostrophe tells us who is owning what. 'Its' never has an apostrophe or else it would say 'it is'. Write the whole word, then the apostrophe. Apostrophes don't touch any letter.

Copy the owner's name under each picture.

Megan's pony tail.

Ravi's football boots.

Its wings are patterned.

The child's sweets.

The man's car.

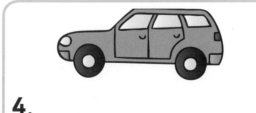

1. _____

2. _____

3. _____

4. _____

5. _____

How did you do?

Homophones and near homophones

Homophones are words that sound the same but are spelled differently. Remember: 'There' has a 'here' in it. 'Their' has an 'heir' to inherit the throne in it. 'They're' has an apostrophe to remind you the 'are' is missing. 'Hear' has an 'ear' in it.

Match the homophones. The first has been done for you.

there here son see sea bare hear
their one bee sun night two to bear
be blew blue knight won

spelling 1	spelling 2
there	their
knight	night

How did you do?

Spot the errors

Shape? Size? Sitting on writing line? Joins?

Circle the mistake. Write each word correctly.

sink	sink	
well	well	
Germany	Germany	
brother	brother	
sister	sister	
swing	swing	
queen	queen	

How did you do?

Change the size

Which size do you like best? Tell your teacher!
Use your fingers to move the pencil, not your whole hand.

Copy these patterns.

Write your name in big and small writing.

How did you do?

Fluent writing

Remember to join. Joined writing can help you to remember better.

Revise for your weekly spellings here.

1.

2.

3.

4.

5.

6.

7.

8.

9.

10.

11.

12.

13.

14.

15.

16.

How did you do?

Well done!

Cut-out your reward Ollie.

Name:

.... Theo ....

You have completed

Handwriting

For ages 4–7

Age: ...... 9 ......

Date: ....